Poetentialisticly:

Purging Memories

Tina Taylor

For someone else. . .

Read at your own risk and don't be fooled by the cover. This book contains a reality I wouldn't wish on my worst enemy. It contains subject matter that may be triggering for some, and I hope that anyone triggered or struggling with mental illness will reach out to someone because you are important, and the world needs you.

Authors Note

I have to say I've learned a lot from baring my soul to the universe. Not everyone receives honesty gracefully and many turn their backs and close their ears at the slightest hint of it. My poems are not about specific people but rather certain types of people and are often fueled by pure empathy for someone else's pain. Being free from the metaphorical grips of my monsters is more important than winning their affection and I'd rather eat alone than swallow poison. I hope to free others in the process.

I've also learned that there are entire communities of people just like me who shed their pain through poetry. It not only helps us to heal but it shows others that there is still hope and no one is truly alone. Keep fighting the good fight. You're worth it!

Contents

Poetentialisticly:

Purging Memories

Another random collection

of poems

Written by Tina Taylor

a.k.a : Ninjapoetica

Writer for a Million Voices

I hear it all the time

with almost every poem that I share

Both women and men say "I can

relate to that" or "I've been there".

And my heart breaks for all of them

because I know the amount of

strength it takes

to hold your tongue and put on a

smile for someone else's sake

I know it isn't easy and how the

words stick inside your throat

How bad you want to break free

from it

but you don't want to rock the boat

I hope with every piece I write

I open a door for someone else

The world is full of broken people

trying to fix themselves

But every poem I write, I write for

you

Please know that you aren't alone

Embrace your broken pieces

because they are proof that you

have grown

Footwork

Another piece of me died today

as we sat face to face

While I fought to hold myself

together

my heart fell from its place

Now it rests in pieces

at the bottom of my feet

So, every step from here on in

the damage is done by me

Numerical Anchor

If the scale measured me based on

my health

the number wouldn't be the same

If I could get the number out of my

head

maybe I'd be less ashamed

I know what my body has been

through

and why it feels this way

but I still hesitate to get undressed

each and every day

Always comparing myself to others

wishing to be a different size

nervous to go out in public

and be judged by wandering eyes

I think back to when things fit

and I was happier with my weight

but I had to make a choice

because the risk was just too great

That scale gives only numbers

it doesn't know our stories

people tend to be the same

and for that I'm truly sorry

If I could reprogram my scale

to measure in a different way

to understand my battle

it would tell me I look great today

If we could close our eyes

and see only with our hearts

the numbers would disappear

and true happiness could start

The scale doesn't measure beauty

and it's not worth dying for

Don't let yourself be a number

when you can be so much more

It Still Hurts

I remember all of it

The details haunt me to this day

Every moment of my childhood

feeling more like work than play

Always walking on eggshells

because anger rarely sleeps

Hiding my disappointment

for the promises that didn't keep

Folding like a sweatshirt

whenever she came near

I was just a helpless child

silenced by fear

I remember being whipped with

extension cords

and ducking flying objects

Wondering 'why keep a child

you have no intention to protect? '

I remember her bony knuckles

smashed into my thigh

and how her anger grew

because it made me cry

I'm cursed with vivid memories

and emotionally scarred for life

It still hurts but I learned from it

the difference between wrong and

right

Coping Skills

(Part One)

I was already 20 in a 10-year-old

shell

No time for dreams while living in hell

Begging and praying for a way out,

carrying weight of emotional scars

and self doubt

heavier than what I could physically

lift

Tell me again how life is a gift

When they were asking "what do
you want to be when you grow up?"
I couldn't imagine getting there
because I had already had enough
I was tired of pretending that things
were okay
Tired of being coached on what to
do and say
Tired of being misunderstood
Tired of feeling like I was no good
If I could be anything, what would it
be?
10 years from now where do I see

me?

My classmates didn't hesitate to

answer

Dreams of being doctors,

astronauts, and dancers

Living in fancy houses with big

families

Trips around the world and cocktail

parties

I tried to stay neutral while I

searched through my brain

There's got to be something fit for a

stain

For everyone else their dreams

allowed them to touch the stars

But I fumbled for a way to hide my

inability to see that far

And what kind of question is that?

What do you want to be?

At 10 years old I barely knew me

But it had already been years since

someone stole my virginity

Something I couldn't talk about

because who would believe?

As a small child I tried to get help

But for everything that was wrong I

blamed myself

I couldn't say what needed to be

said

I kept the poisonous parts inside my

head

If I tell them the rest of it

and they don't take me away

what are my chances of living

to see another day?

As the years went by my thoughts

swallowed me whole

I lost interest in learning and was

unable to set goals
-
I saw counselors, therapists, and

psychiatrists

But without the missing pieces I

couldn't be fixed

I've been pat on the back for being

strong and brave

For not turning to substance to

numb the pain

But I don't feel worthy of such

praise

For how often I have considered just

leaving this place

~

The rain brings to me

a kind of comfort

not even the sunshine

can understand

~

Black Sheep

I patiently await the day that my pen

touches paper

without bleeding descriptions of you

You who have shunned me for

speaking the truth

When I first started writing you thought

it was cute

but that quickly turned to shame

when the words revealed you

and now me being a writer is

subjectively taboo

You said my poems were like a diary

that should be kept hidden from

prying eyes

because you didn't want people to

know the truth to the lies

You didn't want to be faced with

what you couldn't face yourself

even if it was detrimental to my own

health

And I recoiled to your lack of

encouragement

but continue to be what you resent

The truth of my story still bleeds

through my pen

and to this day I still cry for love I

was deprived of back then

Even though I know what never

was can never be

and you will never accept the writer

that is me

Minus One

You stood there like a hero

And watched the tears fall down my

face

As they tried to take away my

choice

To protect a child from this place

You stood there like a hero

As I took all the blame

Too heartsick with the variables

And the truth too harsh to explain

They tried telling me what's what

But didn't have all the facts

They didn't see what I saw

And still see as I look back

It wasn't that I was too young

Or unprepared in every way

When he asks about his father

What am I to say?

Of course, you're not the only one

to blame

It was my fault too

But what everyone else thought was

best

I didn't think was the right thing to

do

You stood there like a hero

Clueless to the gravity of the

situation

Most likely a result of your actions

But I left you out of the equation

I have to live with that choice

For the rest of my days

I'll always have questions

Of 'what if it had gone a different

way?'

Fragments

I was never popular

but I wanted to fit in

They made it look so easy

I didn't know where to begin

In search of admiration

things only seemed to get worse

I was the butt of all their jokes

and treated like a curse

As suggested by a classmate

Purging Memories

I took a pair of scissors to my face

I would have done anything

to be in someone else's place

I spent more time in counseling

than I ever did in class

Everything spinning out of control,

not even sure how I passed

By the time I reached high school

I was like a turtle to its shell

Suffering in silence,

trying to accept my isolated hell

I took a tool from my math set

and cut into my skin

Torturing the fractured soul

they couldn't see within

I was sure that she had failed me

and we'd never get along

She wasn't worthy of protecting

but I couldn't be more wrong

I owe her an apology

I know I let her down

I was wrong to join the bullies

who laughed as I let her drown

How could they even know?

Would they even care?

The place that she called home

there was no love there

Two separate lives between school

and home

I didn't speak of either to the other

I could barely tell the difference

between my classmates and my

mother

These are just bits and pieces

with which I've built my shield

Although I'm getting stronger

I might never fully heal

It took me years to realize

it wasn't me I needed to fix

It was wrong for me to think I could

make friends

with people who throw sticks

No Sanctuary

They were someone else's children

Someone's daughters and sons

They were meant to grow up

They were supposed to have fun

Buildings for prayer

Topped with steeples

Referred to as God's house

but built for the people

A sanctuary to many

to protect their souls

while those who held the cross

were busy digging holes

They took advantage of their position

Used religion as an excuse

No amount of apologies

could cover the abuse

These horrendous acts of violence

have brought our country shame

and falsified our anthem

by playing a Cowards game

My heart breaks for all the families

and those robbed of their lives

May they finally find some peace

now that we've uncovered the lies

Blue Days

Perhaps today is one of those days

You struggled to get out of bed

You had planned to go out and do

something

but you're stuck inside your head

You can't help but notice the silence

as you drown in the chaos that it

brings

Behind a door that only opens from

the inside,

holding a phone that has forgotten

how to ring

You're at war with your emotions

Your thoughts have grown thoughts

of their own

You know that people love you

but for reasons unexplained you still

feel alone

Take deep breaths and gather

yourself

but don't linger there too long

This darkness is only temporary

and it's not where you belong

Surely this isn't the first time

you've been here

You've gotten through this patch

before

Close your eyes and think of

something else

or maybe someone that might help

you open that door

Remember this, if nothing else:

You're worth so much more than

what's in your head

and if you can believe in yourself like

I do,

perhaps tomorrow, you won't

struggle to get out of bed

Coping Skills

(Part Two)

I sat in office after office with no

answers in sight

Unprepared for a battle only I could

fight

Sometimes it got messy because it

forced open wounds

That spread to cause more damage

when opened too soon

As a child I was trained to be an

emotional vault

Being a people pleaser seemed to

be my default

There were imaginary figures and

stories we were brainwashed to

believe

Yet to lie about the truth was

considered deceit

And even worse was to speak of

what I had seen

Or express how I feel without

sounding mean

But as a child my existence was just

background noise

It would be years before I'd find

courage to use my voice

As a teen I was diagnosed with

depression

My reward for silence and another

lesson

Broken skin on top of scars from

self-mutilation

Punishment to myself for being

human

I didn't mean to be a writer it just

happened that way

I could have used my life as an

excuse to throw it all away

I could have buried all my pain with

toxins and aimless days

But I picked up a pen and started to

write what I couldn't say

With every poem that came out, a

part of me healed

But the weight of what I carry still

feels unreal

This is how I cope with my unfiltered

mess

They might just be words, but they

help me hurt less

So, with a quivering pen I continue

to write

And hope someday my words will

become someone else's light

~

I am thankful for my past,

not because it happened,

but because I learned from it

~

Tina Taylor

Plea for Warmth

I find sorrow in your absence

It lingers outside my bedroom

like a silhouette of my own existence

It mocks me

and gives off such a chill

that my covers feel like concrete

slabs

It drains me of my energy

and leaves me feeling helpless

Perhaps tomorrow

the sun will come out

41

It Won't Go Away

Is it a crime to want something that can

only be yours?

Is it wrong to want to be alone?

Is it too much to ask that you live

your own life and not someone

else's?

If I die would it make a difference?

Would anyone care or just forget

and move on?

If I did my best would it make me

happy?

If I succeed will they leave me alone?

If I fail will I be ignored?

Am I being selfish?

Does it really matter?

Is it my fault I feel worthless?

Is it me who belittles myself?

Or am I being PUSHED?

How long before the pain stops?

How many questions do I have to

ask myself before I reach insanity?

Does anyone know?

Does anyone understand?

Is anyone there?

I hurt! Can anyone help?

Is there a cure?

Or is it just time for my heart to

stop. . .

Stop hurting

Stop thinking

Stop laughing

Stop crying

Stop hearing

Stop seeing

Stop understanding

Stop beating

More Than Just a Puzzle

Each piece of the puzzle

represents my soul

It's only when they're separated

that I truly feel I'm whole

For when it's pieced together

it only belongs to me,

but for every piece I give away

I'm setting someone free

It Matters

I am not a black hole

But you threw fire without

constraint

Ironically, others worship you

As though you are a saint

Second chances were woven in my

heartstrings

Like the stars are to the sky

You stole the light from every one of

them

Just to see your reflection in my eyes

You never made apologies

You barely covered your tracks

You assumed all would be forgotten

And never find its way back

I've reduced you to a poetic

description

and tossed it to the universe

Never again to cross my path

Or travel in reverse

I am not a black hole of sadness

but a supernova of beautiful

memories

Of surviving your ferocious comets

With my ninja like qualities

The galaxy embraces me

Its warmth is music to my soul

And all that really matters

Is that I am not a black hole

Childless Mother

Empty chairs, quiet spaces

Unread books and untied laces

Broken dreams and thoughts all

cluttered

The struggles of a childless mother

Work obsessions to pass the time

Overly concerned for others' lives

Endless distractions for the

paranoid

There is no cure for this kind of void

An uncontrollable need for

connection

Trumped by the constant fear of

rejection

It is an ache like no other

An empty life of a childless mother

Lost

A world of broken dreams

and many lies

leaves a child in tears

as a part of her dies

Her parents divorced

and went their ways

as the child's future

turned into a maze

Her dad stopped calling,

her mom pushed her away

She felt so neglected

with nowhere to stay

She finds herself begging

for places to sleep

She feels like a burden

No love is for keeps

Will she find hope?

Will she be okay?

Maybe tomorrow

but not today

Tina Taylor

Would You Listen?

The way I feel inside

is so hard to explain

Who has the strength

to understand my pain?

Could I talk to someone

just to tell them my story?

Tell it without crying

or saying I'm sorry

Would I be complaining

if I said my life was tough?

Would I sound like a wimp

53

if I said I've had enough?

If I find the strength to tell someone

how often I really cry

Would anyone listen

if I could tell them why?

No Expiration

I can tell your mind is occupied

Things aren't quite okay

So, I thought I'd send a hug or two

to get you through the day

I know they're only words

more like an I.O.U.

You're free to cash them in

whenever you're feeling blue

You can call me up for coffee

morning, day, or night

Even if I don't have the answers

for how to make things right

Perhaps you're feeling overwhelmed

It seems like the world is crumbling at

your feet

You're not ready to give up

but you feel like you've been beat

You wouldn't wish your pain on

anyone

but you hope you're not alone

I'm here for you if you need to talk

Just please pick up the phone

Note to Self

If I could go back and warn myself

this is what I would say

"Only you can protect you

from what might happen today

Let your voice be heard

Don't be afraid to say no

If something doesn't feel right

pick up your things and go

Don't let anyone tell you, you aren't

worthy

for jealousy wears a disguise

It's often the ones we love

that are willing to tell us lies

Don't claim responsibility

for what you do not own

Keep your chin up off the ground

and know that you're not alone

You have the strength to beat the

odds,

let nothing hold you back

It's okay to slow your pace

but don't you dare step off that

track

Live only for your dreams

and reach up for the stars

Be true always to yourself

and love you for who you are!"

~

I found my voice at the tip of my pen

No band aid can fix what happened

back then

But holding it in can lead to combustion

and only I can save me from this self-

destruction

~

Infidelity

He said 'let this be a lesson

for when you find yourself a guy

I'll teach you how to please him

There's no reason to be shy'

I closed my eyes and froze there

as he helped himself to me

though the darkness couldn't save

me

from the things I couldn't see

Silence has been my enemy

My life a walk of shame

No good deed can free me

from the weight of all the blame

Object

What I thought was a simple act of

kindness,

was a trick to opening my door

Looking back, I see I'm just an object

for those desperately looking to

score

'Please let me get that door for you

while I gaze upon your ass

Wondering just how easy you are

or if you're truly working class

I've already creeped your Facebook

and saved my favorite pics

and before the day is through

I'll send one of my dick

I'll talk it over with my friends,

they'll creep your profile too

Then we'll all place bets

on how long it takes to nail you'

To the guy that followed me home

from school

when I was just a young girl

I still feel like I'm being followed

but I'm more guarded for this world

To the guy that followed me down

the street

in a big blue panel van

I rarely leave the house now

without a pen and paper close at

hand

To the guy that so selfishly used me

for what he wasn't getting from his

wife

you only have yourself to blame

for what's become your scattered

life

Despite what you might think of me

I'm not a damsel in distress

I'm not looking to be taken care of

I don't want to be your next mistress

That life that waits at home for you

is something some can only dream

I think it's time you opened your

eyes

before it becomes what used to be

Tina Taylor

Red Storm

I cut myself open to relay a message

in a language you couldn't

understand

So, you slammed the door in my

face

instead of reaching for my hand

I can't blame you for your reaction

I know it's difficult to see

What's even more difficult

is knowing what lives inside of me

These memories I cannot run from

A past I cannot erase

This hell that I am chained to

You cannot save me from this place

There's no band aid for this wound

of mine

No cure for being broken

A prisoner I will remain

until the truth has been spoken

Gone

You left me in an empty house,

no hydro to light my way

You knew what you were walking

into

but still you went away

By myself, still a child

trying to make it on my own

Feeling like a nobody

Living in nobody's home

Depression Swallows

So often I feel all alone

as if no one in the world cares

and the things that used to seem

important

become nothing, everything is unfair

All the doors around me seem

locked

All the windows appear to be closed

The sun has drifted so far away

To people, I will never again be

exposed

Suddenly there is no color

My world is shaded only in black and

gray

There is no more for me to endure

and I hold no memories of yesterday

To the outside world, I no longer

exist

I never did and I never will

My urge for success tends to fade

My rights of freedom are no longer a

thrill

So, 'what's it like to be me?', you ask

It's like living in a very cold, black

hole

There is no possible way to escape

and the way I pull away now is

beyond my control

Wishful Thinking

I used to have a better imagination

I used to imagine people as better

versions of who they were

In the silence between the beatings

I imagined he stopped because he

actually loved her

I imagined inside the angry man

A sad boy trying to hold him up

Weighed down by his inability

to free himself from the corrupt

I imagined being the goose

In the duck, duck, goose game

When picking for group projects

I imagined them calling my name

I imagined forever friendships

and loyalty earned by trust

I imagined an endless family

made equally with love and lust

I imagined the house full of laughter

No tears or broken dishes

No emotionally scarred children

praying for miracle wishes

I imagined it possible to win love

If I was diagnosed with cancer

It would teach how valuable our time

was

I was sure it would be the answer

.

I imagined being wrapped with love

Without any hesitation

But all I see now is reality,

the reality that your love was just in

my imagination

~

Selfish are those who fail to see

how truly selfless one must be

to say goodbye

~

Lessons

You were our first lesson of survival

Your patience shrunk shortly after

our arrival

Our first reality check of what cold

and cruel felt like

We learned how to fall before we

got on a bike

Four-foot bodies with 3 inch welts

Caused by extension cords and

leather belts

When having troubles with our

homework you refused to help

"It was given to you, you do it

yourself"

Broken children with stitches and

cigarette burns

In a house where love can't even be

earned

You were our first lesson of how

hard things could be

When you react or respond to

things you shouldn't see

We would bow at your feet, not to

worship you

But to avoid your rage filled swings

and things they would do

We tried fixing ourselves to make

you proud

But that's something we would never

hear you say out loud

You were our first lesson of self

defense

Don't enter a room when the mood

is tense

Tears must be silenced before they

hit the ground

Feelings buried, never to be found

You didn't encourage our dreams or

ambitions

But instead made comments and

bets that were somewhat vicious

You were our first lesson of what to

avoid

Without any triggers, you were

always annoyed

You were our first lesson on

predators and prey

As soon we got a chance, we all ran

away

I hope you learned something from

all of that

As I move on with my life and never

turn back

To the Me of Tomorrow

Yesterday I learned another lesson

of how promises aren't for keeps

When you look back and think of me

will you be able to sleep?

Will you take my lessons with you

and make the best of what you

know?

Will you be able to keep moving

forward

without really letting go?

Reflection

When I was just a kid

meals were served at the table

Outside entertained us

because we couldn't afford cable

We were sent to school with lunches

in brown paper sacks

and when times got real tough

we had to bring them back

Before we left the house

our mother often warned

what happens in her house

remains behind closed doors

I was escorted to the office

where children's aid was waiting

to question me on the villainous role

our mother was playing

Sitting in a room full of people

who think they know my story

never knowing what I did

I was always first to say "I'm sorry"

I lied through my tears

terrified to wake the angry beast

I said "she never hurt us"

but the truth had already been

released

I didn't know what made her so angry

or why I always thought it was my

fault

It's so hard to be a kid

when you're the target of an adult

We went to family counseling

as was strongly suggested

but five minutes in

she got tired of their questions

"They just want to know our

business,

they don't want to help"

She didn't want to admit

the issue was herself

Removed from a situation

labeled a potential danger

temporarily placed

in the home of a couple strangers

Why they always took us back

I will never understand

but at least I've learned some

lessons

first and second hand

Like ripples in a pond

abuse flowed through our home

I was still just a kid

when I moved out on my own

I try to keep in mind

that this won't happen again

They can't hurt me anymore

I choose how this ends

Look

When I look at me, I see an unarmed

warrior

standing tall despite the silent battle

that fills her days

I see a capsule of memories that has

added time to her face

When I look at me, I find it most

difficult not to look away

When I see the way she looks back

at me

I know she's not okay

When I look at me, I see broken

pieces reattached but slightly

rearranged

A story long from finished reaching

for another page

When I look at me, I see a damaged

child staring into space

and I so badly want to tell her that

we are both the same

That our vessel is not meant to

drown in a sea of pain

That the possibilities are endless

and we have everything to gain

When I look at me, I see an unarmed

warrior ready to face the day

Tina Taylor

The Final Straw

She spoke of our childhood

with tears in her eyes

How when she wanted to hold us

her requests were denied

Children held together

by braces and casts

What kind of future

would emerge from this past?

We were to be ghosted

neither seen nor heard

She'd heard of tough love

but this was absurd

She had no idea

where this hatred came from

If you can't stand children

then why be a mom?

As the years went by

the visits became less

They were shunned for their

questions

Tina Taylor

about our abusive mess

Then came the day

I showed up at her door

All grown, on my own

and held captive no more

We kept each other company

I tried to visit everyday

but her children found it offensive

and tried to keep me away

She cried out of frustration

not knowing what she did

She was blind and all alone

bullied by her own kids

I kept up with my visits

and we bonded so well

So many memories

she had so much to tell

They sold all her things

and put her in a home

confined to a chair

and left on her own

It was there she gave up

and how could I blame her?

try as I might

I could not save her

I knew the last visit

was the last indeed

and 2 days after that

she was finally set free

~

I don't hate the people who have

hurt me

as deserving as they may be

I hate the way I see people because

of it

and how I see me

~

Introspection

Our lives are full of obstacles

but we do the best we can

It may be hard to reach our goals

but we keep them in our plan

As long as we have support

the hills won't seem so high

The mountains may not move

but will be easier to climb

Many pieces of my past

have tried to slow me down

but I keep taking bigger steps

Purging Memories

to keep above the ground

I used to be the master

of holding everything in

but I learned it feeds the darkness

that lives beneath my skin

I'm still picking up my shattered soul

from the love I've never had

with a hope that someday soon

my life won't seem so sad

I'm still searching for myself

in a world I left behind

by processing the memories

that are poison to my mind

Tina Taylor

This is me still trying

and I hope it won't take long

to find myself through all this mess

and maybe right some wrongs

Safe Zone

When I was a young girl

I strapped rollerblades on my feet

Turned my back on the chaos

And found my safe place in the

streets

From morning to nightfall

I rolled through the city

Took in the outdoor breeze

Before returning to the land of

shitty

Every day for longest time

Tina Taylor

My rollerblades were my escape

Even now I can feel it

How my rollerblades kept me safe

But isn't that ironic

How the place most known for crime

Is where I found peace

and spent most of my time

Even the places we once lived in

No longer hold negative vibes

Like they did when I was a child

Knowing what lived inside

A Girl's Pain

I remember this small child

just a little girl

Lots of pain in her heart

reaching out to the world

A world she quite often

didn't want to be part of

Was it such a bad thing

to want to be loved?

There were a few people

who gave her some hope

but afraid of getting hurt

Tina Taylor

she rarely spoke

of what happened some days

behind closed doors

that brought her to tears

as she wondered 'what for'?

Afraid to cry out loud

too scared to speak out

Just a little girl

always wanting out

What's left of that girl

is a lot of pain

Many years later

she feels it again and again

Still reaching out

but no one is there

They probably can't see it

if they did, they might care

Tina Taylor

Distraught December

When I think about December

it often makes me sad

to think of what it used to be

and the love I thought I had

How we gathered at the table

and shared a holiday meal

Now the chairs are empty

and that is what I feel

The presents long forgotten

Loved ones who have passed

My only wish for Christmas

is that it goes by really fast

Purging Memories

I don't miss the decorations

or sitting around the tree

What I miss, I cannot buy

that's the feel of family

All the walls that have been built

and the ties that had to be severed

These are thoughts that cross my

mind

when I think about December

My hope is that my sorrows

will only be my own

and when Christmas morning comes

no one will be alone

New Year's Efforts

It's about that time of year

when we tend to set new goals

Time to build new bridges

and bypass all the trolls

This year I'm going to do it

This time I'll get it right

This isn't like the last time

This year I've got more fight

I know I say this every year

but this one's not the same

Last year I wasn't ready

but now I've brought my game

I'm going to take smaller steps

careful not to slip

and if things get rough, I promise

I won't abandon ship

I won't set the bar so high

that I quit before I begin

I won't give what I don't have

I won't sell my dreams for fins

This year I'll keep it simple

and do only what I can

That way there's no disappointment

if things don't go as planned

~

Sometimes words can heal a

wounded soul

if you lay them out just right

Some hugs hold all the power

needed

to calm ones' restless night

~

Toothpaste Mangler

Who used the toothpaste last?

What has it ever done to you?

Why do you feel the need

to squeeze the center of the tube?

Have you no basic knowledge

of how the toothpaste works?

To get the best results

you squeeze the bottom first

To squeeze the center is just lazy

and asking for a mess

as it could come out the bottom

and now there's even less

Then it'll probably be everywhere

except where it's meant to be

You'll have to change your clothes

again

but after you brush your teeth

Before you brush your teeth

take some time to think

A mangled tube of toothpaste is as

frowned upon

as toothpaste in the sink!

Indoor Sky

In this world of mass pollution

I have found a temporary solution

to be able to see the stars

Though they aren't quite the same

and some might think they're lame

at least these are not so far

The lights of the city

Tina Taylor

diminish all that's pretty

but my stars still glow

Above my head in the night

in my room when there is no light

my sticker sky will show

300 stars up for admiration

may be lacking in constellations

but they still bring me peace

As I lay beneath this glowing

with my inner child showing

I can fall asleep with ease

A Small Request

They said "girls are supposed to

wear dresses"

but they don't understand

that sometimes it feels like an

invitation

for boys with bored hands

I can't tell them what happened

They'll say it's all my fault

and of course, I'll believe them

because I've never heard of assault

I wasn't being difficult

when I said I prefer pants

I can't undo what's been done

but I still deserve a chance

To think a dress could haunt a

woman

over twenty something years later

because "girls are supposed to wear

dresses"

no one thought to save her

Now she's told she should be

flattered by compliments

and could have any guy

but she just wishes people could see

her

without opening their eyes

Please take this memory for what it

is,

a lesson to be learned

The reason children have voices

is because they deserve to be heard!

Letting Go

I am ready to let go

of a past that made me weep

A past that seemed to haunt me

each night that I did sleep

The many times I watched her cry

for the bruises on her face

Every time she felt alone

because she felt like a disgrace

I am ready to let go

of the pain deep down inside

The pain that told me I'm not good enough

to have my parents by my side

The many times I waited

that he didn't even call

to say that he was sorry

for not showing up at all

I'm ready to let go

of a past I cannot change

A past that broke my heart

and locked me in a cage

I'm ready to let go

of a pain that made me run

The pain that robbed me of my childhood

The pain that told me they had won

I am ready to let go

of the hatred that I've held

because they never seemed to try

to understand how I really felt

I really want to try now

to start with moving on

Let go of all the bad things

Let the past be gone

Life is just too short

to keep standing in the shade

You have to open your eyes

and let your past just fade

Hearts and Chains

I know you don't like to talk about it

and things aren't how you wish them

to be

but you owe it to yourself to open

up

and set those demons free

You don't owe her your silence

You don't owe it to them to get

along

You're allowed to be angry

for the things that they did wrong

As much as you say the past is in

the past

I know it's not what you believe

I know how hard it is to give a love

you know you'll never receive

Locked up in a bedroom

with windows nailed shut

You deserved to be loved

and got everything but

Brother, you don't have to tell me

I can see it in your face

You're worried what might happen

if you empty out that space

You cling to your demons

because of the titles that they hold

but when you needed them the most

they left you standing in the cold

I understand where you're coming

from

I tried to fix things too

but sometimes holding on

causes damage we can't undo

Brother, I know you're hurting

and your heart bleeds for something

real

but you owe yourself the freedom

of expressing how you feel

We were only children

forced to grow up way too fast

We don't owe them our future

for contaminating our past

I want you to know I'm proud of you

and I see how far you've come

but you don't owe it to them

to pretend to be numb

Dear brother, I still love you

and you should do the same

You don't owe them anything

and you don't deserve the pain

~

If I reach for the stars

and only end up with a handful of

leaves,

at least you'll know I tried

~

Solo

I feel like I'm addicted to darkness

because it seems to be the only thing

that's consistent

Something no one else wants

so I can't resist it

And in that darkness lingers a

mountain of memories full of

childhood trauma and insecurities

The building blocks that were

supposed to help raise me up

Tore me down to the point of not

giving a fuck

At least not out loud and not where

they can see

I'm disconnected but at least I'm free

Common Misconception

I hear you don't like my attitude

and I can't help but be amused

You've mistaken this for a friendship

I see how you'd be confused

So, let me spell it out for you

Y-O-U space A-R-E space P-H-O-N-Y

I'm not programmed to pretend

I don't care enough to lie

They like gossip here far too much

to keep it all low key

Everything that you have said

has made its way to me

I work out of necessity

We don't cross paths by choice

I don't owe you any courtesies

I'm not afraid to use my voice

You don't have to like me

but there's no need to be a jerk

After all, I'm not here for you

I'm only here to work

Clarification

You read it in the papers,

people who've been bullied to death

You wonder just what were they

thinking

before they breathed their last

breath?

'Why does this keep happening?

How did we miss the signs?'

They were there, believe me

but you chose to close your eyes

You preach about zero tolerance

but to whom does it apply?

You place the bully on a pedestal

while the victim is questioned, why?

Maybe that's not what they meant

Maybe they're having a bad day

Maybe you should just ignore

the things that people say

You call it isolated incidents

So, you're not at all concerned

That's like saying it's okay to be

bullies

as long as we take turns

Often, we are punished

for standing up for ourselves

We are forced to pay our union

dues

but we can't force them to help

So, preach about zero tolerance

as freely as you please

But your words, they hold no

meaning

because it's actions that we need!

One

This is a tough subject and I'm not

sure where to begin

but if I'm being honest

I'm ashamed of my skin

I didn't ask to be part of this club

but I want the fuck out

I want to stand on the rooftops

to scream and shout

How the fuck does this make you

better?

What is this really about?

If every racist being was robbed of their

eyesight, they would see

The only difference is in how you treat

other human beings

Put 1000 people in a building with

blindfolds on their face

There would be a rise in

communication

instead of a war on race

What happened to equality?

I thought we progressed

What are you accomplishing in all

this mess?

The hatred, the violence, unjustified

deaths

This isn't the answer, take a deep

breath

Take a moment to think of where

we're going with this

Listen to the universe

Did we really come all this way

Just to hit reverse?

You can't blame everyone for the

actions of one man

We're all just surviving the best we

can

Cowards feed on violence and hate

There's a cure for ignorance it's not

too late

If we stand together, we'll persevere

Fight with love and put an end to

fear

Put down the weapons and stop

passing blame

We are all different, but we are all

the same

We are One

Stories

He interrupted my reading

to ask if I'd read a story from the

bible

Something of a famous man

and what are known as his disciples

I told him I don't believe in it

though I thought I did before

Of course, that piqued his curiosity

and he asked that I explain a little

more

If such a god did exist

we wouldn't live in chaos and

destruction

run by the rich and greedy

polluted by mass production

I don't believe one who creates life

could so heartlessly take it away

Grant children to abusive mothers

Allow the beauty of the earth to

decay

I don't believe there would be

unwanted children

or people dying in the street

Places where food is thrown out

daily

while other places have nothing to

eat

When people are feeling desperate

they get on their knees and pray

to the same god they cry to at

funerals

for taking their loved ones away

I think that god is an acronym

for something as simple as Grow Or

Die

No story can convince me

that there's a god up in the sky

We all believe in something

We've all been dealt a different

hand

It's up to us to take control

and live it the best we can

I'm sure it's a fascinating story

but that's all I believe it to be

As far as my story goes

the only one I give credit to is me

Stored

My mind is an endless storage facility

It holds enough memories

to remind me for a lifetime

that your absence is the key

And not all of them belong to me

But still somehow trigger my ptsd

Like the tire swing in the front yard

You laughed as the boy was spun

Knowing full well he wasn't haven't

fun

You even called him names when you

were done

You took humiliating photos and told

him you would show all the girls and

they would laugh too

you told him they "would never want

someone like you"

You took us to the cemetery down the

street and nearly scared him off

his feet

Then made fun of him for not being

able to sleep

Being made to stand outside

In nothing but his undies

while the rain disguised his tears

Your abuse was far from funny

His windows were nailed shut

And the door locked from the outside

Knowing he had a habit

Of starting fires inside

Unexplained scars and broken bones

No wonder your house was never our

home

Maybe you were tired or struggling

with something we couldn't see

But if a child's existence makes you

angry

Why have 3?

My mind is an endless storage facility

It holds enough memories

to remind me for a lifetime

that your absence is the key

And not all of them belong to me

But still somehow trigger my ptsd

It would have been nice to have a

childhood

That doesn't require a lifetime of

recovery

Tolerance

You give me the stink eye,

suspicious I might be infected

I can only hope you catch what I

have

and may your mind be redirected

Though I'm familiar with the

situation

and the panic it has caused

I haven't forgotten we're all human

and fear is the worst of our flaws

I understand where you're coming

from

and I brush it off with a smile

I can only hope it's contagious

and finds its way back into style

Put on your mask and gloves

Do what you need to do

but don't forget you aren't alone

We're all human too

Just because you can't tell by my

expression

it doesn't mean I do not care

I don't feed into the fear

I don't have the energy to spare

All I can do is smile

and silently wish you well

Perhaps one day you'll return it

when we've beaten this

pandemonious hell

~

I'm tired but I can't sleep

I'm hungry but I can't eat

Another poison memory that won't

seem to end

The only way to slay it is by picking

up my pen

~

Tina Taylor

Riddle Me This

The doctor asked a question

to which I could only respond with

tears

but how do you summarize suffering

that you've been drowning in for

years?

They've called it chronic sadness

They've told me I have depression

Yet their total lack of answers

has me questioning their profession

Purging Memories

They scribble a prescription

based on a two-minute diagnosis

further imprisoning me

in this emotional psychosis

I don't need a bottle of "cover up"

I have a box of band aids at home

What I need is a real support system

so, I know I'm not alone

I don't need to be told how I got

here

for the pain is still quite fresh

Tina Taylor

What I need is a real solution

to free me from this mess

Our resources are lacking

We struggle but we try

We need a better army

to fight the demons deep inside

We're told to let it go,

that it's all just in our head

Compassion doesn't surface

until someone turns up dead

Even then there's waiting lists

sometimes followed by hefty costs

If we don't have the funds to please

our files just get tossed

So, doctor, please, answer me this:

Where do you draw the line?

Is money really more important

than the chance to save our lives?

Sugar Coat

Love, unconditional, forever, family

Words I associate with everything

opposite reality

Today is family day

My sister told me to tell

how awful my family is

but she has no idea

of the life I have lived

I feel sorry for her

The family I was born to

would rather pretend

there's no truth to my story,

there's nothing to mend

I feel sorry for them

I'm related to a bunch of people

A few of them are nice

I try to keep my distance

So, they don't pay the same price

It's not easy to stand alone

I told my dad how I feel

and now we don't speak

He was aware of the abuse

but turned the other cheek

I feel sorry for him

It must be difficult to run from

something

that's not chasing you

To expect one to be honest

without speaking the truth

I will not be silenced

I won't apologize for this

I won't apologize for me

We might be related

but we are not family

And I . . .

am NOT sorry!

Chances

One

Two

Three

Young and stupid

Not ready

Write offs

Turn the back and let time pass

New tree

New leaves

Many seasons later

One

Two

Wait for it

One

Fail

Two

Last chance

Last resort

Last attempt to prove

what a good dad you are

Say What?

Sometimes she said "I love you"

but she had a weird way of showing it

Sometimes she said "I love you"

but it always felt empty

Every question was answered with

anger

Every touch was fierce

Sometimes he said "I love you"

but it was usually followed with a

lengthy absence

Sometimes he said "I love you"

but all the words before and after

were full of insults

She said she loved him even after he

put her head through a wall

She said she loved him after many

bruises, sprains, and tears

Every time I hear the word love

I feel the weight of emptiness and

confusion

I've been told many times love will

find me

but for what I know love to be. . .

I hope not

Even in Death

Today I am of sound mind

but tomorrow that could change

I want to make myself very clear

in case my life gets rearranged

Remember that time I asked for

help?

you said to apply for assistance

Well, here's your reward for your

generosity

and acknowledging my existence

Tina Taylor

Don't waste your time lingering in my

doorway

if you hear I've fallen ill

I don't owe you any courtesies

you're not included in my will

For all the times you came to the city

but didn't stop to say hello

My gift to you is my absence

So, you can stick to what you know

All my material possessions

will be given to those in need

because even when I'm dead

I won't stimulate your greed

No point in crossing your fingers

for any money left behind

It will be donated, every penny

to a charity of some kind

As for me, I can rest in peace

knowing there's nothing left for you

to take

I've lived my life and left my mark,

this last wish is not a mistake

~

May my absence open your eyes

in ways my presence never could

and may karma show you mercy

like mother nature would

~

Broken Valentine

We weren't among the lucky ones

I don't wake to the pitter patter of

feet

Every Valentine's day I'm reminded

of a heart that doesn't beat

Every day I struggle with my reality

some dreams aren't meant to come

true

Maybe I was just selfish

to have only wanted you

For 22 weeks we were connected

in a fight we couldn't win

I was living in denial

of what was happening within

At 13 weeks we lost your heartbeat

but I had hoped that they were

wrong

You stayed with me until Valentine's

day

as if this is where you belong

There are days I can't lift the covers

and wish that I could die

just to see if it's possible

to meet you on the other side

I know it's not realistic

We can't go back to the start

So, every year on this day

all I see is empty hearts

Birth Control

I strongly believe I was a case of

misconception

and my parents are probably wishing

now that they had used better

protection

I don't think that they'll read this

I don't make them proud

They don't like that I'm honest

or write so loud

They don't like being reminded

of the mistakes they've made

They don't want credit for the price

I've paid

Like the abandonment issues

that grew from his absence

I know that nobody is perfect

and shit happens

I called him from payphones and

rented cars

But he always used excuses like I

lived too far

Gas is too expensive

He doesn't have time

Yet when I don't call on father's day

he wonders why

Sometimes years go by before I talk

to him again

And it's always the same cheap

blows that I can't stand

You look just like your mother and

you sound like her too

and I want to ask him

"Should I be more like you?"

He doesn't know the details

and he prefers it that way

What happened back then

or who 1 am today

I'm sure it's no coincidence

that there's a hurricane name after

her

most who cross her path have been

made to suffer

with side effects like depression and

ptsd

Complete with a lifetime of things

that can't be unseen

Like all the times she dragged me

along

to her booty calls

so no one would suspect she was

cheating at all

I'm expected to hide my feelings just

to spare yours

and provide open windows to

replace the closed doors

All the time that has passed and the

Purging Memories

lessons I've learned

I don't have the energy to rebuild all

the bridges you've burned

They probably blame me

for why we can't get along

because I refuse to pretend

that nothing is wrong

And I've been told I need to be

the bigger person

to forgive and forget

as if one can swim

without getting wet

They tell me to let it go

that I've blown it all out of

proportion

But it's because of them

that I believe in abortion

I don't have the strength to hold

myself down

I crave air too much to let myself

drown

Quite often I think about dying

but it doesn't mean that I don't want

to live

It's just that I'm exhausted

and have no more fucks to give

I don't care that we're related

or what family should be

I can't pretend that I love them

when I don't feel they've ever loved

me

I refuse to put out a welcome mat

to absorb their every excuse

Or any reasons they use to try

to justify the abuse

I won't harbor vacant spaces

in case they grow up

They've had ample opportunities

and I've had enough

I don't love them or hate them

I'm not angry or sad

I'm no longer wasting wishes

for what I never had

I feel like they're incapable of growth

and I've never been the child

All these years of failed attempts

I see no chance for reconcile

I hold myself together

I walk my own path

No credit to them

I've got my own back

If my parents ever read this

and have any objections

then they should have made better

choices

and used protection

Regret

I am sorry

I don't know how to fix my face

in such a way

that when you look at me you can't

see her

I'm sorry you can't speak to me

without feeling resentment

You said you're just a donor and

called me a write off

yet I still make the effort to include

you

But most of all I'm sorry that when

your words play over

and over and over in my head even

20 years later I still feel defective

When people compliment my

qualities

I can't help but to respond with "it's

a birth defect"

because I have never known either of

you

to have qualities worth such praise

Your absence and her abuse did not

teach me how,

but how not to

My existence is inconvenient for you

and I'm sorry, but did you ever for

one second think

that your decision to fuck her was an

inconveniénce for me?

One day I hope that when you look

at me

you'll see me for who I am instead of who

I'm not.

Vilified Love

I have that kind of memory

Sometimes a blessing but mostly a

curse

I remember all the details

Love and hate unevenly dispersed

Being made to feel worthless

By those who say I deserve better

An object of convenience

All business and no pleasure

Only an idiot would love me

I often believe those words he said

Even on the days I don't

They still linger in my head

These memories now invisible

passengers

People I knew or know

The ones that talked of love and

forever

But didn't hesitate to let me go

I have to talk myself down quite often

From the ledge those memories push

me to

Memories of being told to kill myself

Wrapped tightly with feelings I can't

undo

No matter how much time has

passed

Or what has happened in between

I still can't help but wonder

If what they said is what they mean

All the words spewed out of anger

From all those 1 have ever loved

Mixed with the lies of 1 love yous

No push left to defend the shove

Some days 1 feel 1'm ready

That it's time to hit eject

From this life that doesn't want me

And the love 1'll never get

1 know 1'm quite impossible

And can't fix the damage done

But I still can't help but wonder

If they'll love me when I'm gone

Tina Taylor

Writing

A thousand thoughts just sitting

like landmines in my brain

It's more dangerous to let them out

than to just absorb the pain

An easier road was provided

but I turned the other way

I feel stronger when I'm struggling

that's why I'm still fighting to stay

I have dreams that seem too big

though they may be petty to

someone else

I often care too much for others

who only care about themselves

The words I rarely say out loud

flow easier through my pen

They do not know me now

as they did not know me then

My words may seem empty

but my pain is very real

I often write about people

and how they make me feel

I see them as they are

and as they could be

I see the world differently

and my feelings run so deep

I write about my life

my hopes and all my dreams

I write whatever comes to me

and about things that I have seen

I often write to relieve myself

of stress I cannot bear

I keep it as a reminder

that sometimes life is not fair

Also, it reminds me

of how very far I've come

and how well I have grown

despite the hatred that I'm from

Observation

I'm not as scared of sleeping

as I am to be awake

People are so selfish

they don't think before they take

Often being questioned

of self-inflicted pain

People don't look for answers

before passing off the blame

Always spreading gossip

Tina Taylor

without an ounce of proof

Amused by ones' misfortunes

too blind to see the truth

Don't Call Them That

Don't take candy from strangers in

the park

Don't wander in the streets after

dark

Don't talk to strangers on the bus

Don't trust anyone but us

because we are your family

Don't take rides from people you

don't know

Don't tell anyone you're home alone

Don't tell anyone where you've been

If they knock don't let them in

Beware of strangers

You demanded the truth though you

taught me to lie

You told me you love me but you

made me cry

You were supposed to protect me

but I never felt safe

When I hear the word 'monster'

I only see your face

I can't think of anything more

strange than that

But I got in the car you told me not

to

And I went in the house I wasn't

supposed to

I got to where I needed to be

and learned what 'family' really means

I did it all against your advice

Tina Taylor

When I hear the word 'stranger'

I don't think twice. . .

because they practically raised me

Best Before

I'm one of those morning people

who wakes in the wee hours of the

night

After yesterday is gone

Before today finds its light

Much like food

I have a best before date

and if you approach me after 7 am

then you're much too late

And I won't be held responsible

for the expressions on my face

in response to your presence

or any sounds your mouth makes

I wasn't always like this

but people change people

Ignorance sometimes looks like

strength

and strength can become feeble

In the morning so very early

I breathe in all the silence

The absence of stupidity

and lack of sirens

For a brief amount of time

I sometimes feel inspired

but then the world wakes up

and suddenly I've expired

~

Who could ever love

a tortured soul like me?

A prisoner to the past

struggling to break free

~

Night Terror

Ancient lanterns hover

beyond the graveyard gates

late in the night where the sound of

coffin scratches

cause a rippling of cemetery chills

and the reaper of fear just waits

Surrounded by bones and bodies

mixed with gargoyle graves

deep in the decrepit woodland

where the demons' slave

plays vampire games

And the eyes between the trees

blink to the rhythm

of the gatekeepers' chains

While off in the distance

you can still hear the screams from

the crypt

in the old, abandoned prison

where the walls are bleeding a

watered red

throughout the haunted hallways

It's hard to believe everything here is
dead

I just stand here observing like a
possessed doll
in a paralysis havoc
too entranced from the view to
acknowledge the spiders' bite
As the devil rides his unleashed
fright train
back to his looming lair
at the end of the night

Welcome Not

It is not cozy living in fear

The side effects are catastrophic

And include hiding behind humor

Just to avoid the topic

It's common for children to think

There are monsters under the bed

But imagine those monsters

Living in someone else's head

Controlling the hands

That tuck them in at night

The arms meant to give comfort

When things don't seem alright

The hands that prepare food

To make them big and strong

The voices that are meant to teach

Right vs wrong

The bodies that we mimic

When we learn to walk

The ears that are meant to listen

When we need to talk

Fear has a welcome mat

That no one can see

Tina Taylor

You don't know you've crossed it

Until it's too late to leave

The bold and suspicious

are turned away

But the young and unknowing

are easy prey

I used to live in fear

But I found my escape

Now those monsters aren't welcome

In my cozy place

Detach

We waited at the door for hours

with our overnight bags in our hands

You must have forgot it was your

weekend

Maybe you had other plans

Mother is in the kitchen

calling you everything but your name

She's angry we're still here

She's tired of your games

Weeks go by before we hear from

you

But this is now the norm

We try to make the best of it

Because you are the calm from the

storm

I don't want to worry you

Or put a damper on our time

So, I don't tell what happens at

home

And pretend everything is fine

I tell you I'd like to live with you

But you say your hands are tied

As much as you'd like to have me

That's for mother to decide

And you know she won't allow it

So, you leave the conversation

there

And still, we only see you

when you have some time to spare

Mother gave me her old cell phone

You were the first person I called

She took it back when she found

out

She doesn't want me talking to you

at all

She says if you wanted to talk to me

That you would call me first

Now I feel like I'm not wanted

But I'm sure it could be worse

I'm seeing a counselor again

I'm in a self-destructive phase

I blame myself for both of you

And I've lost my happy place

She's angry more often than not

She thinks I'm sleeping with her man

I moved out to get away

From these things I don't

understand

I spent years putting in my effort

To build a family bond

But there was never a proper

foundation

To build a relationship on

So now I have finally accepted

That things will never change

I've detached myself from the idea

And released myself from that cage

I feel I'm right in doing so

Because I don't hear from you

anymore

By the time reality kicks in

I won't be waiting by that door

Coffee

To the ones that call others lazy

For buying coffee instead of making it

at home

Allow me to explain something

While you sit up on your throne

Today I bought my coffee

And yesterday too

Not because I'm lazy

But because it's something I need to

do

On the days I don't buy coffee

Tina Taylor

I barely leave my bed

Not because I'm tired

But because I get stuck inside my head

I suffer from mental illness

Some days I struggle to get dressed

But on the days that I buy coffee

I'm truly trying my best

Today you call me lazy

But Tomorrow I try again

And sometimes if I'm lucky

I'll have coffee with a friend

So. . . Yeah! Today I got up

I got dressed

I went out

And

I bought myself a coffee!

Forget Me Not

All the years you worked so hard

pushing me away

All your priorities in reverse

taking for granted everyday

All the time you spent admiring

yourself

while we were falling apart

Yet the day I walked away you

claimed

it was I who broke your heart

So much time has passed since then

yet you have still not grown

You beg for me to come back to you

because you can't stand to be alone

You say that I am dead inside

because I won't take you back

but I know the routine and someday

you'll see

the odds are clearly stacked

So, remember me and take from this

whatever will help you to move on

You won't find me again

because the girl you once knew

has grown and is long gone

Whisper

I'd rather be building memories

of beach houses and sandcastles

Instead, I'm still in this place

surrounded by assholes

To hear the whisper of the waves

instead of machines

To muffle the gossip

I imagine seagull screams

I wish to bask in the warmth of the

Sun

by the shimmering seashore

while the conch shell I hold to my ear

whispers ever so softly

'your dream need not be a dream

anymore'

~

My younger self is still inside

helping me to grow

Together we have learned

that holding on

is essential to letting go

~

Yesterdays and Tomorrows

This morning I realized it's been 20

years

since I sat at someone's desk

and watched my mother sign over her

rights as my legal guardian

to a woman she didn't even know.

20 years is a long time and my memory

still holds the details as if it was only

a moment ago.

I remember conflicting thoughts as I

watched

part of me wondering

"is it really that easy? "

While another part of me wondered

"why did it take so fucking long? "

20 years and 1 still have questions

that 1 can't ask

and feelings that 1 can't not feel.

So, make memories with your

children worth remembering

because the severity of childhood

trauma is beyond surreal.

Instead of focusing on world events

and getting caught up in all the panic

be the best distraction you can

and make the best of this time while

you have it.

So, 20 years from now when your

kids

take a glance back to when times

were tough

their hearts will fill with warmth

knowing

that your love for them was enough.

Debris

I'm tired of hearing they're still my

parents

from people who know nothing

about my life

'One day they'll be gone and you'll

regret

not trying to make things right'

'I'm sure they really love you

and did the best with what they had'

'You're going to miss them when

they're gone

and you'll wish you hadn't been so

mad'

I can lay it all out for you

the things they did or didn't do

but time is of the essence

and who's to say you believe it to be

true?

I wasted a lot of time on anger

I let it change me to the core

I lost sight of what's important

and nearly bled out on the floor

Grieving for my losses

and grasping burnt out stars

No one could grant my wishes

because only 1 know what they are

All my life 1've put my energy

into other peoples' dreams

1 didn't realize 1 was slipping

and fraying and the seams

Several times darkness has

consumed me,

practically swallowed me whole

but it wasn't anyone's job but mine

to rescue my fractured soul

1'm the farthest thing from perfect

1've left a lot of damage in my tracks

I've said and done hurtful things

that I can't ever take back

All the pain I have been given

and all the pain that I have caused

I give no credit and pass no blame

because these are only my flaws

I begged for love from vessels

in which it cannot grow

I asked for the impossible

and pretended I didn't already know

But the time has come

I must accept what truly is

Only I can control what happens

Tina Taylor

from here

and hope to grow from this

It's Just Not Me

I don't use filters to smooth my skin

I don't stand in front of the mirror

wishing I was thin

No make-up or fake add-ons in an

attempt to make you blush

It's just not me; I don't even own a

brush

No frills, sequins, ribbons, or bows

No romance novels or soap opera

shows

No dresses, nylons, or high heeled

shoes

I prefer to rollerblade, and listen to

the blues

No aimless wandering in shopping malls

No freshening up in public bathroom

stalls

No desire for diamonds, chocolates,

or flowers

No thanks to profit parties or baby

showers

It's just not me; it's not my thing

I prefer BBQ's, bonfires, and

chicken wings

You can take me out, but I don't

dress to impress

I'm just me; nothing more, nothing less

Excuse This

Your words hold the knife

I'm just here to bear witness

of the punishment to this body

for lacking what you consider fitness

I've been called "sensitive"

and told "people have bigger problems"

Let me ask you this,

Do you think publicly shaming people

will solve them?

People starving themselves on purpose

trying to fit your ideals

swallowing your insults and jokes

instead of scrumptious meals

You call it encouragement

and act like you're doing a favor

But your macho ego is toxic

and lacking in flavor

Your words cut like a knife

and I should want to punch you in the

mouth

Instead I feel sorry for you for having to

work so hard

just to love yourself

Systematic Failure

All too common is this phrase "the

system is broken"

So many children slip through the cracks

It's a shortage of compassion

not resources we lack

Children in abusive homes

are often overlooked

They're trained to hold things in

They live on a hook

Those who sit alone at recess

with their backs against the walls

The ones staring at their feet

while walking through the halls

The doodlers, the daydreamers

hushed by the promised demeanor

The ones that pay attention to their

classmates

and try to follow suit

Nothing out of place

No obvious clues

The kid who sits closer to the teacher

to muffle the whispers of the rest

Seems to listen intently

but still fails every test

Or the ones who have answers

but are too shy to speak

that are considered socially unacceptable

and often labeled as freaks

Children bounced from home to home

being made to feel even more alone

Housed by people only interested in the

check

Who don't give proper care but demand

respect

Children too scared to speak the truth

out of fear that they'll be given back

They often feel unwanted

and keep their bags packed

We're sometimes complimented on our

resilience

as if we had other choices

We wouldn't have had to be so strong

if fear hadn't silenced our voices

The system being broken

is a lame excuse

Made by the people who make money

from children being abused

And we're told to forgive our abusers

"Children don't come with instructions"

If you need to be taught not to beat

children

you are the source of corruption

And the system will always be broken

as long as it's run by greed

It's the ones that have walked in those

children's shoes

that know what those children need

~

A poet's heart

bleeds ink in a way

only a poet can see

and until the poem

is written, the poet

cannot be free

~

Tina Taylor

I've Got This

The alarm hasn't gone off yet

but I lay here wide awake

Many questions still unanswered

Which path am I meant to take?

I'm haunted by my childhood

Weighed down by every loss

but I must keep pushing forward

and show this illness who is boss

One foot before the other

though I feel the tension in my chest

I must prepare for another day

and do what I do best

I put my feelings in my pocket

and force myself out the door

I focus my energy on surviving

but I dream of something more

I know my dreams are only mine to

dream

and no one can take them away

So, through gritted teeth I give it my

all

to make it through another day

I remind myself of where I used to be

and how I've never been this close

How many times I almost gave up

but this is the path I chose

Yes, the road has been quite bumpy

but there is no end in sight

Today is mine for the taking

I'm strong enough to be my own

light!!!

Acknowledgements

I have a lot of people to be thankful for, but to avoid leaving any out or giving wrongful credit, I'll keep it mostly nonspecific.

I'm thankful for the people who have come into my life by chance, intervened with the best intentions and have gone out of their way to show me that kindness and compassion are not just words in the dictionary.

I'm thankful for the mothers who opened their doors, set an extra place at their table for me and encouraged me to make my own path with the stones that have been used against me. I admire you all for the kind of mothers you are, not only to your own children, but to the ones that cross your paths

I'm thankful for those who have supported me through the healing process so far, as messy as it has been. I know it's not easy to wipe someone one else's tears while holding back your own.

More specifically, I owe a lot of thanks to my artist who has gone above and beyond to turn the chaos that is my mind into art for the covers of my books and the tattoos that remind me how beautiful broken can look. Without her, my collections would probably remain loose leaf piles scattered throughout my living space.

I am thankful beyond words.

~

If my broken pieces are what you need to
fix yourself, then please, allow me a
moment to gift wrap them

~

Poetentialisticly

Poetic ~ Potential ~ Realistic

Printed in Great Britain
by Amazon